Splendid State of Mind

By: Eric Walton

Copyright © 2014, 2016 Eric Walton

All rights reserved.

ISBN: 1494745186

ISBN-13: 978-1494745189

The Album Credits

Splendid State of Mind
(God, E. Walton)
All songs and lyrics inspired by God
Songs and lyrics written, arranged, and performed by E. Walton unless noted by *()

Introduction: Golden Moments

Invocation
*(Contains a replayed sample from the book "Wisdom of Sirach" Chapter 41 verses 15-19)

1: Magnum Opus
Beautiful Handwriting
Tears of Joy
Gold Thrones, Green Couches (Splendid Clientele)
Open Ear of Deafness (Interlude)
Stringed Instruments

2: The Precious Moments
The Highlights of Living
Fresh Breath Mints

3: The Dawn of the New Day

Transitional Thought: Test the Water

4: Steer the Vessel
Success Travels (Prelude)
Sail Free

5: Success is a Journey Away
Worth the Weight
The Beautiful Struggle

6: Gold

Transitional Thought: Fresh Fish

7: Thoughtful Consideration

8: The Helping Hand

9: Love's Harmony

Transitional Thought: Genius Fine Line Insanity

10: The Precipice

Benediction
*(Contains a replayed sample from the book "Psalms of Solomon" Chapter 17 verse 43)

Introduction:
Golden Moments

We are spiritual creations by divine design. It is our destiny to become all that God hopes and longs for us to become upon the very moment He creates us.

Whether or not we choose the proper direction is the matter at hand; whether or not we seek the proper course of action down the right path is yet another.

There seems to be a disconnect that is prevalent in this day and age, truth told the day and age before the current as well; weakness is often associated with being in tune with a sense of spiritual consciousness, weakness and even insanity for that matter. If you express this and others along these very lines, the outlook is tenfold. So it becomes a natural adaptation of sorts to compartmentalize it all; too many times people hide it for whatever reason, conformity being the most obvious that I can think. Honestly this can be easily described and seen with a love shared via the expression of feelings; vulnerability becomes prevalent, then for reasons that the bottom falls out so to speak leaving a mind discombobulated, a soul defeated, and a spirit crushed.

Trust me, I have been there. I am still there at times.

No one wants to go through life depressed and downtrodden from what essentially is a broken heart. No one wants to be ridiculed for what is expressed sincerely from the heart. Too many times the voice of reason is unheard by the unreasonable.

We are not created to all be alike; however we all have the same spirit that created us. Compassion and effort are alike, talents are not.

So with that said, I continue to suffer in my passion for the sake of enlightenment and God's glory most importantly. Rather, I continue to be what I am used to being:

Humble to not place myself above anyone below the heavens but wise to know that I indeed am chosen to be a rare jewel.

Superb and unique personified.

I stand alone in my splendor of brilliance.

All for love; the perfection for which I strive, that being the warm embrace of all of the happiness which I seek forever and have had in my mind for quite some time.

God willing that day comes. Lord knows my heart seeks such a success so I can finally rest easy.

These are the up and downs of my life; the peaks and valleys, the highs and lows.

This is divine education that life truly is.

These are golden moments…

Invocation

Have concern for your good name. For this will continue with you, more so than a thousand precious and great treasures.

A good life has its number of days, but a good name will continue forever.

Sons, practice discipline peacefully. For what use is there in either concealed wisdom, or undisclosed treasure?

Better is the man who hides his foolishness than the man who hides his wisdom.

Yet truly, have respect for these things which proceed from my mouth.

Magnum Opus

Beautiful Handwriting

The brilliant is the light shining bright bringing forth the glory that disregards darkness.
When one gazes upon the clear night, one does not behold the darkness then marvel and rejoice.
No! One gazes upon the captivating glory of the stars, beholding the moments of resplendence of each star.
No two stars are alike though similarities exist. The degree of shining light differs amongst the stars; different stars have different brilliances.
The darkness is not at all capable of such beauty; it only is the backdrop for such beauty.
Such is the case of the glory in which brilliance shines; the brilliant being the stars, the shining light through the dark moments and times, a beacon of hope and inspiration for those wandering in darkness.
The testament of the brilliant is written in the sky for all to bear witness; the story of the stars forever etched in the celestial scroll of forever.
God displays His favor for the brilliant with such beautiful handwriting; His splendid and wondrous script of excellence provides light to all below the heavens to clearly see the benefits of love and display love for all who achieve the strive for perfection and ultimate quest for success.
The moon is the grace shining divine light of appreciation, gratitude and love; enlightening memoirs of brilliance written above the clouds. God's shine can never be surpassed; however, God provides your shine as a supreme resplendence of Himself, the supreme achievement for which we all should strive wholeheartedly.

A fool cannot see the light but the wise has the light in the eyes and is never blinded.

Tears of Joy

The brilliant is a plush green field of life basking in the glorious sunlight of grace and watered by the excellence of wisdom.
God's shining greatness and the tears of joy shed by the ancients and the angels in rejoice is the love that gives the brilliant nourishment, sustenance, and vitality; the life and glory in honor of the right path traveled, providing the needs to plant the seeds for others to achieve.

Gold Thrones, Green Couches (Splendid Clientele)

Alarming at my best
Charming at my worst
Harming myself to be the best so I win the prize and net the purse
To taste the sweet success

I endure the stingers
For every painfully passionate struggle
The success lingers
The fragrance of amazement
I salivate to taste it
Impatient in my nature
I gravitate to greatness
The blood, sweat, and tears wiped with a cloth of grace
So I can see crystal clear and understand my proper place

Rise above from the love
Not a higher height shall be acquired in spite
Gravity will indeed humble the mind floating on pride

I ascend to the higher heights
Yet there is a conundrum in my function
Dumping excess as I cleanse my mind viewing the world below
However one's trash is another's treasure
And I truly treasure the trash I dig deep through to find joy and see crystal clearer
Then discard it and wipe the dirt off my mirror
The successful vessel steer
Going full speed ahead never needing the rear view mirror
Riding the wave, staying afloat, letting the water carry me
Carefully
So why should I look back and live in the past
Being consumed with those that place last
Last I checked I am ahead in the race
All and everyone behind me confirms this is my proper place
This is first and foremost so I suggest you catch up to come with me
Not to be a hot dog
Make haste, come swiftly

The plush landscapes
The crushed grapes
Peace establishments, pillars of strength
The calm and serene comfort in the scenic views
Refreshed by memories of the finer art we choose
Report the good news

I was driven by the will to succeed and I arrived safely
And it was no accident
My purpose fulfilled greatly
My drive to golden moments in a gold Benz
Breathtaking visions with the effect of cold winds
Old friends reunited sitting on gold thrones and green couches, inspired
Fine linen, rare jewelry weighing extreme ounces, delighted

Silver linings reign in the color purple
Bringing life to a dynasty of this brilliant circle
Bronze sculptures fitting of this luxury deluxe
Chair cushions and the tablecloth, a matching velvet crushed
Ceramic dishes, dynamic enlightening, the best wishes
Beds of rice provide places of rest for fresh fishes
Sitting at the table in the finest wardrobe draped in a fine silk robe
Delightful moments a magnum opus shall we bask and behold

See joy crystal clear…

Open Ear of Deafness (Interlude)

Deaf to society's screams it seems I listen to the music of my mind in real streams extremely conscious of a classic that is mastered surreal beams of thought enlighten all to the works of art who God is writing lightning fast strikes impact bring thunderous applause for true artistic brilliance

Stringed Instruments

The brilliance of my heart is a song of songs playing eloquently within my mind and it is soothing to my soul
It is a beautiful joy and a fine crystal
Both angelic and pristine by divine nature
The song of angels over harps and other stringed instruments
Stringing together fond memories of a forever that is a long time coming
Both of which I am forever grateful
The forever made easy to locate upon the excellence of the love shared
The love that best achieves the ultimate satisfaction
A testament of happiness written and performed splendidly

The Precious Moments

The Highlights of Living

The highlights of living come after being in the trenches where the lights are low and the outlook is rather dim.

To endure the struggle,
To be an inspiration,
To accomplish what is deemed impossible;
These ensure that shining light enlightens all of an open mind when beholding the full extent of brilliance and excellence

This is just the story of my life
The script of which is written with a gold ink pen
The sheer emotion of joy setting motion a picture perfect praise
A record of reel life plays a never-ending story of my legacy
Vividly displaying in the zenith
Exclusive clubs where those can gain an inside look by simply paying attention

So please stand and witness beyond the horizon
Farther than the naked eye can see
Utilize insight and intuition
Both of which make up the vision clothed in the wisdom of the ancients
Perfectly dressed, presented in royalty to master the appreciation of divine arts and crafts
The arts and crafts utilized to sail free to the final destination
The journey seen and the course stayed
The joy of seeing the process plays out from start to finish
A scenic view of the highlights in the zenith of the never-ending horizon
Gracefully separating the top and the bottom crystal clear
The highlights of living can and shall be watched forever

Fresh Breath Mints

The air I breathe is of a crisp nature
The sensations of the best fresh breath mints
Relaxing and soothing to the senses
The very gust of wind tingle the spine of the wind chime in the brisk winter weather of the Swiss Alpine
The result is a lovely harmony of a sweet success
The best success served on a silver platter
Distinguished from everyone else
Prepared just for my likeness
I shall then savor the moment on platinum plates

I shall then bask in the glory of golden moments
My consciousness fed to the fullest in streams with food for thought
I shall be a well refined testament of brilliance for all to witness the Lord's excellence
His works are wondrous by nature
I am blessed beyond measure to be a chosen few of such brilliance

The Dawn of the New Day

The high that I feel from what I have accomplished is the eagle's nest above
The peaceful and proper perspective of my place of rest mentally
A vivid imagery of the landscape from all angles
The angels send my vision in every direction
The joy of the victory as I grasp the crystal chalice
My celebration is the champagne tears dousing my visage

My cup gathers the overflow

My crown of waves is the superb and unique ocean view for those embracing me and the moment I arrived
Pouring down champagne in this heartwarming celebration of a treasure
A sincere golden moment
A success immeasurable

My cup gathers the overflow

Embracing and treasuring me for who I am and how I ultimately win for them because I always kept them in my mind
I kept the dream alive even though I was wide awake
Could it be that I was sleep walking?
No! The Lord places them all on my mind
And I embrace His will, understanding this is the proper game plan
Doing what is best for the team
And teamwork makes the dream work
It was no sweat for me to do so
My perspiration is inspiration
The sweet smell of success after playing my position
Be inspired
Aspire as I perspire

My cup gathers the overflow

Successful

A rite of passage never before seen among those present
As I pass through humbly, all eyes are definitely fixed upon me
My presence repairs the broken in heart and spirit
For this I am showered with tears of joy
The fine crystal rains of the finest champagnes as light of a golden sun

Behold this is the dawn of a new day
They all witness my moment under the sun on higher ground

They all witness to those not present
They all witness my rise to glory
They all witness my gift of inspiration that I freely hand to them as it is handed to me
I am motivated to do so as it is done
For I am merely a vessel
Carrying across to a destination for others as far as it takes
They show and prove my gifts and talents as I have
They show improvement in their celebration of my present as I have

My forward thinking and moving forward is encouragement for those to move and think forward
My actions generate reactions
A blessing to my testament of brilliance outlined by the Lord
Sketched in the ambiance of royalty
Never sketchy in any regard
Written in a purple rain from the tears of joy when doves cry
My essence is refreshment
This is to be for I have risen above in love
Yet I remain committed to those below as I touch down on solid ground
I score points with the people for I am one of them
I am grounded as I am elevated
The humble and wise sees the best path to travel due to a higher echelon and improved viewpoint of realities seen and unseen

The proper course of action
The proper course to travel
The proper perspective is due to the rise

The sun lowers daily
And so shall I
Why would I think otherwise and face a wrath where I am set ablaze from the sun in the horizon for all to see
Or I am brought down against my will never to arise another day
Never to have my moment under the sun

The art of success is seeing a better tomorrow
And a better tomorrow is having a memory of a yesterday
Bearing witness to the dawn of a new day
Setting self for the rise daily as the sun
And both are inspired by God

Transitional Thought:
Test the Water

There comes a time when your mind is flooded
Instead of drowning under the current
Go with the flow and just rise with the tide
Don't sink into a funk… You can't just wash that away and you just might be washed away

See the journey
Stay the course
Ride the wave
Stay afloat

See joy and crystal clear

It will all make sense once you arrive

Steer the Vessel

Success Travels (Prelude)

Golden Moments

Envision the hope
And how it floats
The perfect vessel to carry across to land promised
Embark on a journey
Travel wisely
God's speed
Fueled by sheer brilliance and superior excellence
Passion sparks my burning desire, the fuel to move forward gracefully
Set sail to coast smooth to that which I aspire
I dig finding treasure
The gold rush has me on a natural high
Intuition is dope
And my scale weighs a ton easily
Please don't sleep
Standby and be alert
Awaiting the shining moment
Opportunity arises as times of sun rises
The humble and wise shall stay awoke

Defining Moments

Embrace the opportunity of success
Just don't grasp for the wind
Aim for the sun
Get it in your clutches then
Take hold to it
Feel the burn
Exercise your mind and all within

Flashy Moments

Full length Polo trench coat
Root Beer Float
Spilled Moet on the deck of the boat
King David Quote
Made the choice between asparagus and artichoke
Lavender soap
Cleans up my mess
Hopefully I stay afloat

God bless
God willing
Yes!
To success
Thrilling

Let's get after it…

Sail Free

My eyes can see
Far beyond the clear blue skies
The beautiful sunrise
To my surprise
This is my mind
To the highest degree
As I sail free

(Take a deep breath)

Sail free

(Take a deep breath)

Sail free

(Take a deep breath)

(Relax)

And sail free
To success beyond
Navigate the channels of wisdom
The current stream keeps my calm
Tuned in to see joy and crystal clear
These presents of time I truly endear
As I sail free

(Take a deep breath)

Sail free

(Take a deep breath)

Sail free

(Take a deep breath)

(Relax)

And sail free
To the course set for inspiration
Strive for that perfect destination
See myself steer others motivation
Winds of change push me through with ease
Receive thanks
As they shout crystal clear with joy "Go Cool Breeze"

Their elation is my education
As I sail free

(Take a deep breath)

Sail free

(Take a deep breath)

Sail free

(Take a deep breath)

(Relax)

And sail free
To justify my journey
The only matter that shall concern me
As God as my witness
The drive that steers me

For me to witness
Sincerely
As I sail free

(Take a deep breath)

Sail free

(Take a deep breath)

Sail free

(Take a deep breath)

(Relax)

And sail free
To a place of rest
My moment of arrival is to be the best
When it's all said and done in my quest
God willing others benefit from my success
No accident in my purpose nonetheless

As I sail free

Thank God I'm getting there…

Success is a Journey Away

Worth the Weight

The road less traveled is the struggle within self
The blood, sweat, and tears exerted in seeing the road is one thing
The actual travel on the road is quite another
It feels as if there is not enough time
Truth told, it seems as if it is borrowed time
Time that has to be returned anyway
Time that really is not mine in the first place
Time I can never pay back at all

I carry myself with dignity, kindness, and thoughtfulness
But often it seems to get me nowhere fast
Let alone nowhere at all
This burden is the hardest to bear
It weighs heavy upon me
It seems to always keep me down

I know where I am going
At least I have the grand idea of where I want to go
And despite now knowing where I come from
I am not certain how to get there
Let alone if I will even make it there

My mind is soaked in a red sea
Drowning in anger, frustration, and sorrow
My temper flashes floods of raging waves

As heavy the burden is to carry
It now weighs heavy on my mind
Seeping into my very soul
Bearing what seems to be the weight of the world on my shoulders
The pressure to succeed overwhelms me

But suddenly I have the voice ring in my head
It rings clear as crystal
Crystal clear as the stream where nature quenches many a thirst
The sparkle as a sun's light of joy
Telling me this plain as day:

Success is a journey away
Passion is the road less traveled in getting there
Passion is a race

A marathon and not a sprint
Slow motion is better than no motion
And progress is a process
There is no need to rush
And you cannot rush learning
Why live a fast life where you miss many along the way?

True indeed, carry yourself accordingly
With dignity, kindness, and thoughtfulness
And I shall see you through
It shall be my honor to do so
Just believe
And I shall be your guiding light, as I will a helping hand

My hope is the wind that shall push you forward
This is an exercise of spirit
So yes I truly expect your blood to flow
And your sweat to drip

I drain the water that has you drowning in anger, frustration, and sorrow
Taste the water running flush down your face
Is it not salty?
Also the water gathering upon your brow
Is it not salty?
All of which is dripping off of you to the ground which you shall walk
Bringing forth light and life to your every step

Therefore I release and relieve the very pressures that burdened you
You can now carry yourself properly as I deem
The world essentially is lighter for you to shoulder the load
In such I help you move forward gracefully
Carrying yourself across mercifully and passionately

Did I not tell you that passion is an exercise?
Thus it shall work out to the end
I only hope the best for you
The best begets the best

Am I not the one keeping you above ground?

Am I not the one playing a harmonious song for your heart of hearts; growing wiser of the life you are given?
Am I not the one lending a helping hand for your life to have significant value?

So please believe that I will not fail you
I am never one to lie

For that is not in me nor is it my nature
Your passion is my credit
I receive your payment in such on the road to success
You pay what you owe and I receive you with open arms
Justifying the fact that you represent for me

This time is time well spent for you to become golden
A gold standard
A golden moment invested in time
A gold vessel
This shows your time spent throughout passionately was well worth the weight
Timeless golden moment to win a passionate race
You win the gold with gold
And in this you inspire the ones who truly appreciate and have an eye for fine art and talent

So now you know and have become wise of the beautiful struggle
So move out and forward to tell those of this very thing
I have full justification of your faithfulness to do so

Go!

The Beautiful Struggle

Faith in the Lord and faith in self are totally different

I can see myself not making it
I can see myself a failure
I can be heartbroken
I can be on the verge of losing my mind
All of which I honestly have and still rings true to this day

My faith in myself wanes tremendously
I lose sight of my brilliance and excellence
My spirit is in peril
My soul begs for relief
My heart gently weeps
I feel powerless and my will to live seems lifeless

Thankfully faith in the Lord is the lifesaver
The sweet joy to see the journey crystal clear
To stay the course
The Lord's will is greater than I
It is independent of me

Love is the answer and the key to success

The strength key to unlock every treasure
The hope instilled in me energizes me to be successful in seeing success

I do not see a way but the way is revealed to me
Therefore I move out and move forward
Trying my best not to look back
I must see it through as it is my destiny

I easily can become ugly if everything is handed to me on a silver platter
Taking everything that is served graciously for granted
Lying to self truth told
For this is why I have no other choice but to embark and embrace the beautiful struggle
Striving towards the gold
The standard of success
I see
What I need to be

Gold

The love that I receive by God's grace is priceless
A shining crystal beautiful and bright
The power to believe that anything is possible
It is worth more to me than any amount of gold

Wisdom is necessary and by any means should be obtained
Her place of rest is knowledge
However it seems to some that some things are best unknown
This shall never be the case for such is a state of unrest
Knowing the path which to travel to obtain wisdom is a rest gained in self
A meaningful state of grace
I am on the road to success
Clearly driven by the will to succeed
And my success will be having her as my own
A match made in heaven
Only to reproduce here on earth

I believe this to be true:
The open ear to hear the Lord's calling is a testament of success
The ability to recognize the Lord's calling through His vessels of choice is appreciation of art and talent

Tomorrow is God's grace,
Yesterday is God's mercy;
The hope that rests in both is the power of spirit and understanding

As I relax in my state of grace, I picture the meaning of life; drawing the following conclusion:

The sun shines rays of hope
The hope for the tree of knowledge to grow wise in stature
The hope that this tree bears strength for all
The hope that everyone seeking fruitfulness to nourish and strengthen themselves comes freely
The hope that this comfort food for thought gives them confidence in their full and proper understanding the need to fully assert themselves

All of this means the Lord's will is the best hope that one can ever have

One's refinement is the hope gained by another who sees such from afar

A hope for the wellness of another is a thought shared in wisdom
The wisdom is the means of staying afloat

Not sinking in the midst of the surrounding troubles

The hope to believe,
The will to succeed;
Both are a stipend for the righteous
Their value is a bed of crystal
Beaming powerful lights in a radiant splendor
Such a light is the power calling my attention
Opening my mind to the higher heights
A new plateau
A higher echelon
Bringing forth the knowledge to believe that success is a journey away
The proper currency to pay the toll to proceed is the very stipend that Lord gives to see me through

Transitional Thought:
Fresh Fish

Before I only heard of this feeling of finding crystal and joy
Then I came across a map
The treasure laid out right before me
I just needed a ride to get there
Driven by the will to succeed, I ran out of gas along the way
Not one to sit still necessarily
I had to make a run for it despite the fact I was on empty
Heck I needed the exercise anyway
I ran laps around the competition
As I kept running in circles
I was my own worst enemy

Feeling defeated, I came to a standstill
I could not see where I was going for it was dark before my eyes
I could not see the light to save my life
How in the world could I read the map?

I felt hopeless
But then it dawned on me
I was standing still and I was still standing
Throughout everything that occurred

That's a good thing, right?

I did not want to sit still in the first place
Forget being passed and not see it coming
I am too tall to be small
I am 6'2" give or take somewhere up there
So I stand out naturally

All of this after feeling defeated
I was still standing
That is seeing it in a different light
And I have an extra set of eyes on top of these two
I have found the crystal and joy
So I am cool

After thoughtful consideration throughout all that just happened
And me being given a map that did not lead me directly to crystal and joy
I have just one question…

What's the catch?

Thoughtful Consideration

I put up with so much nonsense in life
But life itself is not nonsense

I have been misled, taken for granted, and ultimately misused and used for the sake
and tune of other's temporary happiness, resolve, and satisfaction
Even under the guise that such is to satisfy my own happiness

However despite this, I have been granted life and ultimately used for a bigger picture
and greater purpose
To open the eyes wide shut of those guilty of such actions, whether they are
intentionally ignored or unintentionally done

I see it clearly

The helping hand holds me high up to see far beyond my nose

Shall I be thrown to the wayside by the very ones I love, the very ones who express
they love me, and the very ones who have lots of love for me?
But of course
Their hands are shaky in lifting me up
They must be nervous deep down
Scared to admit the obvious
Obviously they are nervous
For when they let me go I am the nervous wreck
Falling from a state of grace way above my natural comfort level
I was more than comfortable before being pulled upon
My confidence was already high
Their expressions of love got me higher
But alas that was due to being full of smoke
There is nowhere to go but down
And this sudden crash course is a steady depressing one
A steady and swift decline
Very much wrecking my nerves
An out of body experience
As I am besides myself with all that has happened

How could this be done?
How easily I fell for this!
My downfall the very story of my life from the beginning

I see it clearly

The helping hand holds me high up to see far beyond my nose

Help me satisfy my desire to rise above from the bottom
I pray that I come up
I am next to greatness when I get besides myself
An out of body experience
Others who put me through nonsense could not see themselves
Chances are they still cannot
Be that as it may

For they view their own happiness and satisfaction
Albeit at my expense
Will they pay me back?
I don't know
Are they paying me back for something I never bought into at all?
I don't know

What I do know is that I am paying for their mistakes
Paying attention after being held by the helping hand

What I do know is that I see far beyond my nose
My eyesight keen as the eagle
The gold seen far ahead for the winning

The Helping Hand

There is no worse punishment than to be ahead of your time and be a prisoner of the moment because others cannot see it

My captivation becomes my captivity
My uniqueness is used against me
I am tried unfairly by those more than eager and willing to place me in a box
Isolated from common population and shamed by the same
To stand alone is to be alone
My only crime is not being on everyone else's time
And for that I am judged unfairly

I think of how adding two negatives wields a positive result
However two wrongs do not make a right
Though the same will suggest that it makes them even
I still feel the scales are tipped unevenly against my favor
As this punishment of mine weighs heavy upon my shoulders
Confused and trapped in reality of myself

God willing I am set free

Thankfully the helping hand bails me out of the bondage
Giving me reprieve from such
Free from the confinements of my harsh reality
A distant reality at that
I see so much from afar
I am way ahead of schedule
Although my time has finally come it is as if I have been here already

I am the eagle released from the cage
Majestic and royal in all that I stand
The depths of my knowledge is as my vision
A rather keen eyesight and outlook
I need room to spread my wings
To breathe easily and be free
So please let me be

My wings spread across testing the air
The winds of time steadily going against me
Putting up such a fight in trying to hold me back
These gusts a strong fury and effort to yet again confine me

Blowing smoke in my face
Such a breeze might pleasure others

I myself have been blinded by compliments in the past
But now my understanding helps me see crystal clear
And the harsh reality of such is those very compliments were false
And false compliments breed complacency
And complacency will have you sitting in a false reality
And lying in the bed of untruths
If you do not stand for something you will indeed fall for anything
So I stand alone
Remaining unflappable throughout

The helping hand has me ready to lift off
The jewels handed down to me from above reflects my value
This value increases in time
So when time finally does catch up with me
I will certainly be worth more than ever realized beforehand

I am ready and willing for flight
The desire and need to soar to new heights
I need to drop these jewels for others while in the bird's eye view
Leaving something behind for everyone to treasure

Eventually
God willing
Hopefully

My only concern is that what I drop from above in flight will be total waste
However the helping hand wipes that vanity clean away
Removing any and all doubt
Giving me the clarity and freedom to fly high in the friendly sky
To be alone high above while staying grounded
Fully connected with everyone

This is a refreshing and well deserved vindication
The helping hand finally tips the scale in my favor
Removing such a burden from me so I can understand my rise above

I feel free to create
I feel free to seek higher learning

My courage and dignity lets my intuition see my way around and through
Comfortably and confidently
In the highest respect
Strength and wisdom fuel my flight
All I must do is follow the light
The light is my guide to be forever free
My insight is clear as the path to freedom is seen

Even when I grow weary along the way
And I run out of energy to go forth in my travels
Basically not feeling fly at all
I do have the freedom to stand alone
And with that being understood
I have the freedom of falling in love
The helping hand gives the spirit of both

The pureness of falling in love shall recharge and refuel me
God willing
The helping hand shall assuredly catch me one way or another
God willing

There are no restrictions in seeking a higher spiritual truth if you lie in a state of weakness

Please understand there are moments where the only thing that gets you through is a song:

The many trials of life will have you debating yourself whether you are guilty or not of being yourself and not like everyone else
This has always reigned true throughout the test of time; many passed on only to fail one way or another, succumbing to the ills of what clearly is being lovesick or stricken with a broken heart

However, beloved, understand that a song of songs was handed to you by the helping hand from the beginning of love

And love is the answer

Love's Harmony

The test of time had me ready to jump off the deep end
I was flying high through the friendly sky without leaving he ground
But leave it to me to be my own worst enemy
A misstep and stumble with two left feet
I truly fell off not thinking about the right
Is it because I did not know the ledge?
Is it because I did not have the strength to carry on?
Is it because I was so high and eventually had to come down?
Intoxicated by what is toxic and needing a sobering experience?

Or could it be that I was falling in love?

I always thought it was merely in my head
No one else could hear what I heard
It was the music of my mind
A tune playing just to get me by
Just keeping me busy and entertained
I could not hear anything else
Nor did I care to hear anything else
Let alone anyone else
The perfect remedy for such a sick stance
The perfect setup to take the fall
So I played my part as the fall guy
But as I sank to new depths
I had to ask myself

Could it be that I was falling in love?

Sinking to new depths gained a new perspective
I thought I knew
And truth told I did know
True indeed
But the understanding did not exist
It was not the least bit clear
However the deeper I got
The sharper I became
My mind becoming cutting edge technology
Amplifying sight and sound
My hearing and vision razor sharp
A crisp fresh outlook

As high as I was
And to the depths of the fall

I had to ask yet again

Could it be that I was falling in love?

Now whether or not that was the case
I thought that was dope regardless

The deeper I became, the insight cleared everything within me
Then I saw what I heard all that time
The music of my mind was not just in my head
It was an art so picturesque as if it was drawn with a golden ink pen
Drawing from clear and refreshing streams of consciousness
Free flowing to travel anywhere the heart desires
And it was carried and delivered by two angels

These two angels obviously had my best interest at heart
Truly they both are heaven sent
Both delivering such a blessing handed from above
Plus their glow and shine kind of gave it away
Such radiance is a beautiful joy and a fine crystal
The song that they sing is the very actions I experienced first hand
They held me down and kept me uplifted
Each in their own superb and unique brilliance
With the excellence of love's harmony that they sang

This was the very song that I heard
This is what I thought was only in my head
But it was also in my heart
An angelic bliss of a love twofold
It made me tune everything else out
In perseverance and strength all throughout
It was wise to have this play on an endless loop
For there seemed to be no ends to the depths of my fall
Or so I imagined

Through the testy times
And the good times that passed
Love is the answer

It is wise to acknowledge love at all times
In that I am much wiser for having such a love delivered to me from two angels
Both are a blessing to have under each arm for love and support
Holding me down and lifting me up
Both heaven sent and personally delivering me that art which was sent from heaven
How blessed I am to have such blessings!
How loved I am to have such loves!

As tough as the fall was from high above to the depths below
Indeed the worst sinking feeling
I must admit that I am a better person from it
What an achievement in itself it is to grow deeper as you sink to the love below
Being uplifted by the sound of a love's harmony
Drawn perfectly and framed at the picture perfect movement
A truly progressive lifestyle

I am stronger from this because I am wiser
Oh how the mighty have fallen and have lived to talk about it!
My testament of such hopefully etched in stone
Or better yet drawn along the horizon to be seen to the extents of forever
The chance to have my story shared
The understanding of having my legacy learned
I value giving the ultimate respect out of understanding from being wise
By firmly shaking the helping hand

Could it be that I was falling in love?
Indeed it was
Indeed I am
And I shall always embrace such a fall
The lovely angels and the art keep me going from the lovely songs sang
Love's harmony has me floating in air and walking on clouds
The footprints of the wise for all to see in the skies

Never be afraid to fall in love
Let love come to you limitless and naturally as the art it is
It truly can save your life and make your life valuable
It is an exercise of the heart
It all works out for the best in the end

No matter the uncertainty you may have
You are wise to trust love
And in trusting love you shall become wise

If it is right, then feel free to jump
Go fall in love
Achieve new depths to reach the higher heights
You shall see those painful tears be tears of joy
Be worthy of the catch
Trust me
Trust yourself
Trust love

Never did I know falling in love could be such a rush stemming from such a rush of judgment…

Transitional Thought:
Genius Fine Line Insanity

I don't know where I want to be
But I do know I don't want to be here

The Precipice

Beloved, please believe and know this to be true as always:

This which comes forth spoken from my mouth comes directly from my heart.
Love is the wisdom shared, the excellence explained, and the brilliance of it all.

The life worth living

The most impossible thing to realize is that the most impossible thing is not impossible at all
Not in the slightest
For we all fall short of the glory of God
Self included
But we rise above for and with the same as we fall short

I, myself, am a testament of such
My fall was a steep one
A rather sudden descent and swift plummet
However this was by divine design
Though my hastiness and impatience was of my own
Going through the motions I needed a speed that was slow
My peaks speak upon not the ultimate satisfaction
For I was never satisfied
Rather this spoke for the need to achieve a higher height
My attempt to reach the next plateau

Hindsight begets insight

I stood at the precipice seeing flashes of life before my eyes
I stood there to clear my mind
Weathering the storm
Trying to make sense of it all
Searching for the proper perspective of reality
But my perception was stained

Vision impaired from the cloudiness
And my mind the exact same
There was not any depth to my perception
Everything appeared the same
Within reach yet out of touch
My reality felt nothing of course

The best course of action was to jump
To get to the other side

The side I can see vaguely yet I know is higher than where I was
It looked closer than I thought
Perception is reality
Everything was the same, I level to myself
So I jumped

I now learned the depths of reality
The fall taught me well
The perception now is my reality does not exist
The downpour of tears fell as fast as I did
The tears were moments of clarity
As they washed away the cloudiness of my perception and outlook of reality
My vision made easier to see
My mind just as clearer
My outlook that much brighter
With each moment I fell

The depths of my knowledge grows every bit of my descent
Wisdom keeps me from coming to a crashing halt
In this I stay above ground
In this I rise
The fall begets the rise
The embarking of the journey to the next plateau
I rise above to reach the higher heights
Yet I had to come down in order to do so

Giving up and giving yourself up are two different acts
Yet doing one results in the other
God's grace allows us movement,
God's mercy allows us opportunity;
Both power tools for learning and living
Both knowledge and wisdom
Both being brilliance and excellence
Both being life and love.

The journey through life is one where learning is paramount:

One must learn what life truly is
Then one must learn what love truly is
After which can one honestly see the relationship of life and love:
Life poses questions
Love presents answers

Benediction

His words will be more refined than costly gold, the finest...

Splendid State of Mind Bonus EP Credits

Gorgeous Self Explanatory (The Long Story Short)
(God, E. Walton)
All songs and lyrics inspired by God
Songs and lyrics written, arranged, and performed by E. Walton unless noted by *

1: Humbled Beginning
(Destined To Fall)
*(Contains a replayed sample from "Book of Psalms" – Book One – Psalm 37 verses 23-24)

2: Brilliant Contemplation
(The Fall)
*(Contains replayed samples from "Book of Psalms" – Book One – Psalm 38 verses 4, 6, 8, 10, 17)

3: Poetry in Brilliant Motion
The Brilliance Remembers
(Contains samples of "Splendid Tapestry Woven in Excellence" written by E. Walton)

Applies Mathematics (20/20 Vision)
(Contains samples of "Splendid Tapestry Woven in Excellence" written by E. Walton)
(Contains samples from the book "Splendid State of Mind" written by E. Walton)

4: Brilliant Triumph
(The Rise)
*(Contains replayed sample from "Book of Psalms" – Book Two – Psalm 45 verses 1, 4, 17)

5: Gold and Green
(The Higher Heights)
Gold
*(Contains replayed samples from "Book of Psalms" – Book Two – Psalm 49 verses 3-4; Psalm 68 verse 18; Psalm 71 verse 7)

Green
*(Contains replayed sample from "Book of Psalms" – Book One – Psalm 23)

About the Author

Gorgeous Self Explanatory
(The Long Story Short)

By: Eric Walton

Humbled Beginning
(Destined To Fall)

The steps of a good man are ordered by the LORD,

And he delights in his way.

Though he fall, he shall not be utterly cast down;

For the LORD upholds him with His hand.

Brilliant Contemplation
The Fall

For my iniquities have gone over my head;
Like a heavy burden they are too heavy for me.

I am troubled; I am bowed down greatly;
I go mourning all the day long.

I am feeble and severely broken;
I groan because of the turmoil of my heart.

My heart pants, my strength fails me;
As for the light of my eyes, it also has gone from me.

For I am ready to fall,
And my sorrow is continually before me.

Poetry in Brilliant Motion

The Brilliance Remembers

Life

Progressive Growth

Valued Life

Assertive Will

Hope

Faith

Inspiration

Encouragement

Fulfillment

Achievement

Applies Mathematics (20/20 Vision)

Magnum Opus (**Achievement**)

The Precious Moments (**Fulfillment**)

The Dawn of the New Day (**Encouragement**)

Steer the Vessel (**Inspiration**)

Success is a Journey Away (**Faith**)

Gold (**Hope**)

Thoughtful Consideration (**Assertive Will**)

The Helping Hand (**Valued Life**)

Love's Harmony (**Progressive Growth**)

The Precipice (**Life**)

Brilliant Triumph
(The Rise)

My heart is overflowing with a good theme;
I recite my composition concerning the King;
My tongue is the pen of a ready writer.

And in Your majesty ride prosperously because of truth, humility, and righteousness;
And Your right hand shall teach you awesome things.

I will make Your name to be remembered in all generations;
Therefore the people shall praise You forever and ever.

Gold and Green
(The Higher Heights)
Gold

My mouth shall speak wisdom,
And the meditation of my heart shall give understanding.

I will incline my ear to a proverb;
I will disclose my dark saying on the harp.

You have ascended on high,
You have led captivity captive;
You have received gifts among men,
Even from the rebellious,
That the LORD God might dwell there

I have become as a wonder to many,
But You are my strong refuge.

Green

The LORD is my shepherd;
I shall not want

He makes me lie down in green pastures;
He leads me beside the still waters.

He restores my soul;
He leads me in the paths of righteousness
For His name's sake

Yea, though I walk through the valley of the shadow of death,
I will fear no evil;
For You are with me;
Your rod and Your staff, they comfort me.

You prepare a table before me in the presence of my enemies;
You anoint my head with oil;
My cup runs over.

Surely goodness and mercy shall follow me
All the days of my life;
And I will dwell in the house of the LORD
Forever.

About the Author

Eric Walton was born on February 4, 1977 to his parents Robin Walton (nee DeNeal) and James Walton in Gary, IN, specifically hailing from the section known as Aetna; this neighborhood being where he learned a lot of life lessons, gained confidence and positive reinforcement from many friends, family members, and peers of various backgrounds and walks of life.

He graduated from William A. Wirt High School in 1995 and Purdue University in 2000.

Despite being a graduate of Purdue, he considers himself more a student of the art of life and life itself with the hopes that one day he shall achieve a legacy and level of timeless recognition; more important than that, finally achieve the happiness he so hopes and longs.

Eric has one sibling, Anthony Walton.

He has one daughter, Erica Walton, who is resting in peace for she was stillborn on January 19, 2013.

This is his second book written and published; the first being The Rise with Love: Eric Walton in Rare Art Form. This book, Splendid State of Mind, is the follow up and natural progression of the first; both written testaments in the form of albums, seeing that psalms are indeed songs accompanied with music.

This book is a conceptual poetical movement in progression of The Brilliance of Eric Walton (Part II of Eric Walton in Rare Art Form) as summarized in what the Bonus EP is (and thus why the title is such). The progression starts from what really is the end and leads back to the beginning; this is hindsight which gives birth to insight. Additionally, this is written in a way to convey what ultimate is the rise and fall; trials and tribulations; the peaks and valleys.

And this is Eric's battle with depression.

This is a multilayered love story. A story of questioning life and having love answer those questions. This is the process of life and love becoming understanding.

This is the becoming of True Artistic Brilliance, much rather the majestic ascension to it.

Thank You

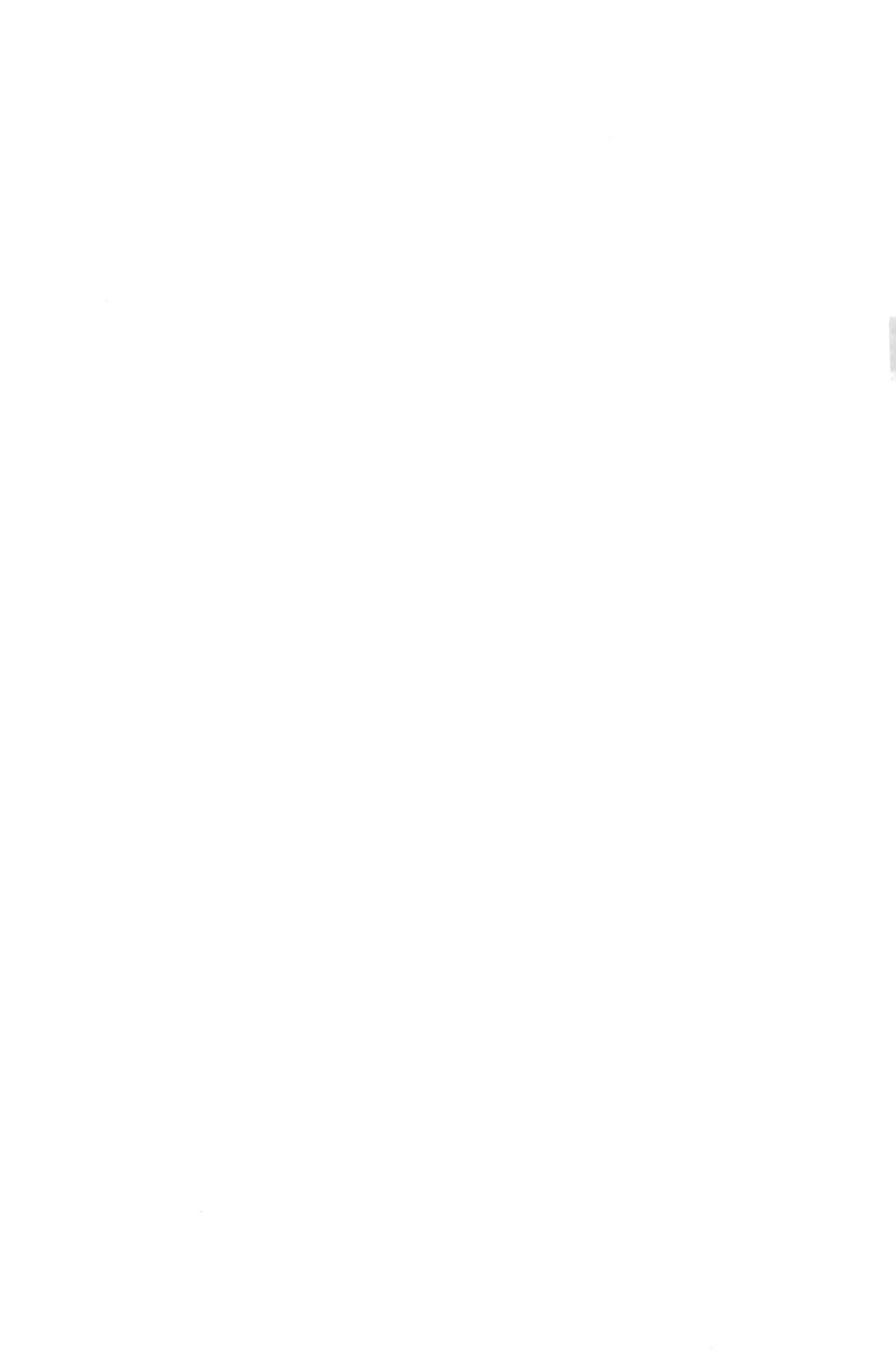

www.ingramcontent.com/pod-product-compliance
Lightning Source LLC
Chambersburg PA
CBHW081739170526
45167CB00009B/3881